Words that forgot
they exist

Dementia Dialogues

Other works by Norbert Ruebsaat

Poetry
Cordillera
A Hog Na'to

Memoir
In Other Words

Plays
La Viglia
Odon von Horvath
Through the Leaves
Faith, Hope and Love
When the Leaves Turn

non-fiction
Speaking with Diane Brown

Words that forgot they exist

Dementia Dialogues

by Norbert Ruebsaat

2019

Acknowledgments

To my sister Rika, who remembers it all
To Jim, who follows truth
To Lorenz, who follows the storyline
To Harvey, who lives in the world of
friendship
To Andrea, whose spirit took me home
To Sonja, who thinks and dances like
the sun
To Hildi, who speaks to truth
To Stan Persky, mentor to my mind and
heart
To Caleb and Caius, my grandsons who
hold the future

Thank you…Rika, Lorenz, Terry, Sonja
For assisting in the book's journey from
concept to physical reality.
For reading the poems, and asking
questions.
For listening, hearing and reflecting
with me.
For encouraging my words.
All of you know my heart.
Your presence holds me like the land-
scape.
Thank you….

INTRODUCTION

This is a remarkable book by a writer who has spent a lifetime trying to capture what it is for one person to truly communicate with another. It is remarkable not simply for the quality of the poems – their clarity and simplicity, the piercing insights and often-painful expressions of self, balanced by a warmth and outreach to the reader that is profoundly moving.

No, what makes this collection all the more important is that these poems are the work of a poet who realizes he is slipping – slowly – into dementia. They are the poems of a man whose brain doesn't work as fast as it used to, and he knows it. The power of the poems lies not in dramatic imagery but in the way they bring the experiences and perceptions of the poet – not muddled but razor-sharp – to the reader. They are, as he puts it, "old guy poems", the fruits of a lifetime of reflection and extraordinarily sensitive perception of people and place – less here the mountains and lakes of the Kootenays (the subject of his other works) but more the people closest to the author – his partner, daughter and friends. All the tools of the poetic craftsman are harnessed here in a work that is as fine and as memorable as anything the author has ever created.

These are poems that invite the reader into a place that will mark him or her deeply, because they speak to a reality that many, if not most, of us will experience as we grow older. If the reader is not an "old guy" (or "old girl") already, then he or she will be one day. And that's why it is important to read these poems today. They show us the clarity that comes with age, the distillation of emotion and perception that is, in fact, a special kind of gift.

This, then, is the poet's gift to us, the readers of this singular collection. It is a sublimely successful effort to show us the next stage of life, and as a reader and friend, I am very grateful for it. ~ Jim Mitchell

TABLE OF CONTENTS

Chapter 1

Chapter 2

Chapter 3

The teenagers who don't
die

The funny one

Chapter 4

Randy

I am the animal

Like two shoes

For this Morning Friendship

The inner voice and the
outer voice

Thinking about something
that is not a thing

The lady in the distance

There is this thing

What is a birthday; a
feeling

Logic and Love

He's thinking; making it up

Chapter 1

Dementia Moment

"If I do this I'll forget what I just
did
What should I do?
This or that?
Who's talking as we speak?"
(The Plan) (The Plan?)
Am I strong or am I weak?
Who knows?
Depends
On what?
Is there a "you" and an "I" in this
story?
One can't make things up.
They do it themselves.
The events.
There are words that don't know
they exist.
Can't remember.
Which?
The executive skills...

(June 2017)

I've been reading your writings

Friend Harvey, key words
His elegant sentences
In hand and man and heart
Yes

Harvey, the event, the experience--
feeling
The story, its reality

Our talk the knowledge
Our conversation
Yes the event
the experience, feeling, the feeling

The story,
the Reality
the knowledge
what we did and said
Believed?

Our conversation
The story
The poem

The "it" The "if".
The knowledge
The sound of verbs and words

A place and location
One is "from" somewhere
Conversation

The conversation with Harvey
The man from many places
The event wants to be known

Do I listen to myself?
The "id" the ego, the super id
The story or the fact
the story of the fact

How do we sing?
The "being"
What's certainty?
or the "not being"?

The man knows his being.

To my Daughter

True meanings
being with you
making us
Loving the reality
with you
Its truth
The places
being us
The touch
we become
Thank you.

Home

What is a family?
A place
where one is with others
With thought and moving
Being, present with
Thought and meaning
and feeling
Attention to the other and one's
self
Where one is.
with love and place and that self
Respecting memory
One has the names
The love one means
Here
PS:
In this place one can be a kick
dancer
a bookwriter and publisher
theatre actor
father and mother and grandma
and grandad
all in one

A daughter and a father
and a place

A conversation
Making the place.
True
Being here
With it
There with us
A location
True
Thank You.

For Sonja Oct. 25 2017

Elder Poem # 58

My Self.
Am I paying attention?
to myself?
Does it pay attention to me?
The Self?
Am I paying attention to myself?
Is my self paying attention
to itself?
His name is Norbert.

Elder Poem # 85

How does one simply die?
What can "die" mean?
For whom?
If at all
Is one there?
A friend asked me yesterday
what my plan was
for the major event
You could have been there or might
be away
In the morning the wolf comes
to chat about your damaged back
The back damaged itself

For Andrea's 65th Birthday

Her walk made me look
To what?
Her stride
The certainty in the foot
The knowledge in the known direc-
tion
As needed
The voice leads well
One pays attention
The "you" that are to me

Yes, I'm in love
Here where we are
A house you led us to
And where the love lives
With its depth and true life logic

Heart is the word at centre
Where you have brought me
Thanks to your miracle birth.

Morning Rhapsody

Here
Side by side
like two shoes
Waiting for the future? Or the past?
Who one is in a partnership
say a marriage
or a love nest?
Who am I as I say this?
You, or the place where we are?

Let's count the possibilities.
Let's talk them and touch them
and be us
here in a home
that lives for us
wants us to be in a place called
here

May 17, 2017

Elder Think and Questions

The woman gives the body
the men take the body
Or other way.
Is the body the culture?
Or is the culture the body?
Who's asking?
And who's doing what?
Answering?
Itself?
What's thinking all about?

This morning the CBC Radio had
under ten-year old children
speaking about their daily lives
in the studio
They spoke, like little adults
in cages
They understood
it seems
what a microphone is
and loud speaker
Technology young
talk
being a future for us.

The Brain Pays Attention

to the pain
to the moment

the brain pays attention
to the meaning of the pain
it tells the story
as far as possible

til the pain comes in again

An Elder Talk - for Barry

I have a sense of continuity with
myself
said a good friend
We still live our story
Who's the friend?
I'm doing the asking
The making?
Given today's ideas
about reality
What can they be
these days ?
So called
By whom?
The platforms on which we produce
our selves
whatever that is?
Ha ha! Who's who?
Laughing?
Up there?
With it.

Here

people live at a camp,
the mountains hold their ground
and lakes,
Their lips lick the water
with its rhythms
the mountains maintain their
meanings
You hold the shore
 At Your Own Risk with the camp-
ing place
says the camp sign
You experience
a place
the harmony
its tone
The tourists speak for themselves
their musings.
The places

Do I dare the spirit?

I'm moved by places
who know me
seem to
would know
the "here"
that the buddies and the partners
(lovers) hold
One wants to be with a "here"
Maybe then, more

July 2 2018

Chapter 2

Being Oneself

It's hard to be myself
says the old guy to himself
Who's who here?
Asks one
and who are you
asks the other
Who's who
they ask in unison

Those two guys
who think they are
themselves
They start to fight
something guys like to do
For space? for place?
Or time?
What's that got to do with it?
Fuck, what's "it" mean?

Okay what's what here?
Who's right?
And who is righteous?

What the fuck.
Isn't that a woman's thing?
asks one of the two boys
the two guys we are talking about.

Say Hey, god damn
who's talking here then
anyway?
Tell the god damn truth
Yeah
go to AA
and get away from the booze
These meetings are a god dam
breeze
when you really think

Do women want to be understood?

Do men?
Who's true?
Sometimes feel responsible for
everything
Often fail.

Most of the men here are boots
after them come trucks

The man voice tones with the engine
The women arrange themselves
then laugh
Men listen to their engines
the women to themselves
the children use their shrill
voices
Life in the valley
Men rumble with voice, Low low

July 25, 2017

Life and Death

Does logic gain
or does sense?
Sensation
What makes us be?
And go?
Here? Are we then?

It hangs around in the brain.

the inner voice. The language
Of what? Who? You?
Remember me already
before you even think
It's not a machine,
the language, the mouth of time
life's clock.
Think about that. Tell it to your
voice.
A word is something we have
Sometimes the voice drinks booze
if you know what I mean.
Can mean.
Without being that way.
Let's go with the heart and the
brain.
that You.
A reader.
A word is something we have

for our life
So to speak.
A word is a thing we have against
death
speaking is listening
listening is speaking

Elder feeling #88

The weather is the event
You might be in the doings
a place you can be a part of

It's all about language
yours and it
Don't under estimate the meanings
Something speaks its language
where you are
do you listen?
Are you part of the "It"?
that abides here?
Are you with it?
You might be present
in the moments
You look outside

February 27 2018

Normal Being

It's not normal to not know what
not knowing means.
I'm not normal, I don't know what
not normal means.
It's not normal to be not normal.
Is it normal to be not normal?
Can it be normal to be not normal?
Who and what?
Am I?
When I'm old?
What do I think I am?
How?
Normal morning.

Words are love

can be
Know you with their sound
from the art where "you" can live.
Right now
the art of it.
Here
the word is the tongue language...
sound

the words tell themselves
always the truth.

He wants to know
I want to live.
The voice is the muscle of the soul

The Art of friendship

I have a friend
he's old
like I am.
We were friends back then
still are.
Do what we then did
When boys were doing this
that friends still do.
It's called love.
the boyish kind
of the "you" and the "me" Type
We know each other as brothers
who seem to have familiar names.
know a kind of world
of our making
a place of talking and thinking.
You are me and I am you
The "You" is always here
at my edge
shoulder...
friends with truth...and mirth

There's some reality here....

Life and Death....

Does logic gain
or does sense?
Sensation
What makes us be?
And go?
Here? Are we then?

Morning aphorism

Do I think or do I feel?
What comes first?
How?
What if?
Who decides, id or ego?
You or me?
It or we?
What is it then, this "thing" that we
think about
Or feel about?
Do I trust?
Me or it?
What if?
Morning aphorism.
Thinking of
the non whatever

Old Guy (Alone)

Thinking about death
Who could?
And how?
If you were dead?

How would it be?
An "it" How could "it" be?
Stupid?
Who do you think you are
anyway?
If what?
Who the hell is talking?

Or is it you?
Yes, let's talk
you and I
whatever.
Forever?
How would "it" be
then
without me?
Or "with"
(Is anyone here?)

Where is the attention?

On the pain.
Who's right about the attention
question?
Where "should" it go?
One needs to be hard
or one doesn't make it, get through
says the woman mother
The son wants to save her from
herself. But always fails
(ease into a sentence)
Does she take out the whip
or does she leave that to the dad
Who's who, whispers the son.
Where is the world? he wonders

You could wander by accident into
the family hell
if one is you, yourself, me myself
and I

You can't control the others
that want to control you.
A coming of age story
of a boy who is an immigrant

A German boy who is an immigrant
and a German Canadian.
Boy, German boy

The pain arrives is it I or you or
we? Us?

When the Germans picked up the
Latin story what did they make of
the new religion?

Want to be the local bard?

What did I always want?
Peace and love and friendship.
What about heroism?

The mother who walks away
her back toward you
you go to prank and fight and war
and addiction

You make a police state
in your head and its world.
You go to sex
whatever now can mean.

sexaholic
and the shopaholic....
How does the man who's love
leaves the room and slams the
door.
What should the man do?

July 8 2017

Chapter 3

For You

When I talk to myself who am I
talking to?
You? It?
If?, a "You?"

Can one think this way?
Does one listen
Or make the necessary noise?
With voice one is one's self in?
What does this mean?

There's no reality
to be had
by the moments
one pretends are present
I'll engage none the less
in the now
Am I?

The man

his teeth are about himself
you can't listen to him
because you... because he...
gives only orders.
His teeth are about himself
How to...when you try to be a
renegade you always
punish yourself
Does he want a companion?
he doesn't take thanks
You might be right
The mountain is the mountain he
doesn't think
The mountain is the mountain
You bet

2
The mountain is the earth
You are there
With him?
Where?
Location
Being when
The mountain is time

told
there
One makes the sign
What is sound?
Louder than echo?

Being the answer

3.
You are not a sentence
Yet. Yet?
When can we talk?
Blending the mountain with the...
Location...? Where can one
be? Up there?
Being a chance
The ruling is in the backpack
The mountain pounds the drum

My dear daughter spirit

The voice speaks
"Us"
Where we are
with knowledge that thinks us
in the place
that understands our hands

in world life

and voice

(who's Norbert when he speaks?)

My everlasting daughter

Dear Daughter
The way you moved yesterday
through your birthday room
the fortieth one
Your hand touching time
and each person present
a family feeling
in each moment
That could be distant too
Indeed as you danced
with sound and around
as food gave its names
to the meanings of us being here
Here you are
as I recall you and us all in that
room
and something sings

Forty - For Sonja

My daughter's forty.
Imagine that.
Just think.
For a while you remember
then you wonder
whose is what it is.
Yesterday she helped me when I
almost fell on the rocks at the Slo-
can Lake beach
I felt little
heard her adult voice
holding.
Her son, my grandson is entering
grade eleven
tomorrow,
imagine that
He told me Wikipedia was more re-
liable than teachers
he preferred books.
His mother was making lunch when
Caleb boy and I talked about the
meaning of "meaning," that word,
and some other ones.
When his mother brought the lunch
to the table I thought of a baby,

my daughter and my grandson
carried, I'd held both.
Being held now
by their time and their places.
I'm here as a memory of
you the reader
and listener

The teenagers who don't die

They live in a valley
that knows their names
They've lived here forever
unmoved by time
but knowing all that's needed.
You could be one of them.
It's not complicated
it's you in other garment gear
You name yourself
without a second possible thought

The truth is not always the same
truth
one is surprised
one is not who one
thought
one is and was
one tries to remember
something
believes
tries to
be something
Could be a valley in the mountains
and a lake

of eternity and time
a circle?
When the creeks creak down the
caves and cliffs
one remembers
oneself
in a "here"
So one thinks
I'm one of them
the locals true ones
the "here ones"
real
Why should we have gone to the
army? they said

September 4th 2017

Old Guy Poem
(The funny one)

The toilet hole
hello
You never know
what when

To do?
With what?
When?
Ha ha

The flush
That's maybe
not always
successful
do

You're old
your
metabolism
Whatever that is
knows you
with its
wits

Ha ha
Kick that flush
haha
You know it all
the 'how'
Those morning rituals

Flush
Don't blush

July 31st 2017

Chapter 4

Randy

He's a man who listens
You listen too
Call it present
Where he is
Location
and place
You've suddenly
Realized
But what?
You ask him again
not with words
so much as with
Presence...Sense?
Who would
this man be
If?
What?
Something about friendship
In your hand with him when
As you think
Not the usual kind of
truthmaker
How he does it is not known
Yes
friendship

One thinks
Not so much truth as with
feeling, sensation
You learn as you trust
A certain kind of silence
True one
He's a surprise

I am the animal

I am the Other
Who am I trying to fool? Ha! ha!
On who? The joke?
Who's eating it?
The truth.
Whatever that is.

Or who?
Are you with me on this?
Are we, say, love?
Could that be
in the truth cupboard, say?
Where that God guy holds out
waiting for truth?
Maintaining it?

You name yourself in a story.

I am the self

May 6th, 2017

Like two shoes

Here
Side by side
like two shoes
Waiting for the future? Or the past?
Who one is in a partnership
say a marriage
or a love nest?
Who am I as I say this?
You, or the place where we are?
Let's count the possibilities.
Let's talk them and touch them
and be us
here in a home
that lives us for us
wants us to be in a place called
here

May 17, 2017

For this morning - Friendship
Harvey

Your voice about them and us
Friendship being heart felt
The story, the poem and the fact
idea (story)
The being with the "other"
here and them
with us

I read your reviews
your heart in place
The text and the hopes
and the sensation "truth"
"we" a kind of "it'
A man who listens
and speaks
from heart and mind
the spirit
The way you blend sound and text
telling and hearing
"it" the "it being" and the telling
and the hearing
The love we know

The inner voice and the outer voice

Who are they?
Who's talking
meaning itself
for whom?
Are you the one?
To whom do I listen?

One wants to be
A "you"
and I?
Or a you?

Or the "it"
the "ego"
the "superego?"
Who am I and who was I?
In the then.

Thinking about something that is not a thing.

What is "it" then?
In the world and here?
Where?
The idea that I am better,
stronger?
Than the other boys

But I may Be fooling myself
No I'm not.
I'm
misunderstood
By myself sometimes.
You, that you. that one
Thinking about something that is a
person
Not a thing.

"You" and a "we"
Here. does time
Exist?
I am waiting. for "You"
There is time and there is death.

The lady in the distance

Who is she
when she calls from the distance?
Hers?

When he calls from the distance
does she know?
The baby doesn't know that he's a
baby
Does she?

Motherwanting
is not acceptable
these days of life

One needs to know this

There is this thing called death

and this thing called life.
These are twins
Who's who?
What's a thing
called something.

One knows nothing
the something doesn't exist
Oh no, it remembers.
You
I'm talking to him
or her.
You
That "it" with us
The "you" and "we"
We believe
I call
A song knows better
about this
"thing" called language
You can draw paint this on a wall
Or if you are a First Nationer
you paint on stone

You carve the true. Truth
That's your own fault
says the saying
laughs or weeps
pretends not to know
HEllOW!
WOW!
the story says
The print you hear
You get punished for what you say
There is this character

I think with reverence to key words
every day
living a wrought root
and rout
The self creates itself

you talk to your self
as if
The program the system
I get greedy for truth
the scientific kind
and the belief time kind truth
framework

Being and meaning (it)

The spiritual kind
of thinking
Here, in a place of knowing
and sensing
sensing? And fictioning

there's no reality
no such thing

November 11 2017

What is a birthday?

a feeling?
a meaning?
Something heard about
as a child
You are in it and think.
About or with it.
Who's talking in it?

Logic and Love

Two things and ideas.
Felt here. Being and having.
Been there and here
when at all

What does love mean?
A dance?
Sensation and language?
Hope and sense.
Being with.

The hope language
The with one with being.
The fire. The thing that makes a
warmth.
It's sound that talks
What can true mean? Really mean?
Then and now?

He's thinking

Making it up
or the truth
or invention?
Who's making this up
the truth
so called
For now?
Til you die?
Who's you anyway?

Words that forgot the exist
dementia dialogues

Norbert Ruebsaat has worked as a writer, translator and journalist as well as lecturer in Media Studies at Simon Fraser University and Columbia College in Vancouver, Canada.

Among his interests is rendering in language the ins and outs of embodied cognition. How it is that we express a sense of place; or the way words move along the tether joining our identity to our (self) consciousness; or seeking for words that no longer know they exist.

Norbert was diagnosed with vascular dementia in 2015, giving him a new subject for his writing skills.

Now retired from teaching, he resides in idyllic New Denver, surrounded by the lake and mountains of the Slocan Valley of British Columbia.

These poems reflect his ability to live in the moment while sharing in the love of his friends and family as they travel with him on his journey.

30353566R00046

Made in the USA
San Bernardino, CA
24 March 2019